REINVENTION

KIM BISSETT
RUTH BERCAW
TERRY KLAUSMAN
ANDREW REACH
PJ ROGERS

REINVENTION

Published by: The Artists Archives of the Western Reserve
to accompany the exhibition of the same name

Designed by: Mindy Tousley
Contributors include:
Kim Bissett
Ruth Bercaw
Terry Klausman
Andrew Reach
PJ Rogers

Photography for Terry Klausman is courtesy of Brad Hart
All other photography is courtesy of the artists or their agents

AAWR Support Staff:
Executive Director: Mindy Tousley
Gallery and Archives Coordinator: Christine Ries

AAWR Board of Directors:
Herbert Ascherman Jr., President
David Joranko, Vice president
Philip Bautista, Treasurer
Jocelyn Ruf, Secretary

Richard Cline
Lee Heinen
Dr Vincent Monnier
Stuart Pearl
Rota Sackerlotzky
John Sargent III

REINVENTION

KIM BISSETT
RUTH BERCAW
TERRY KLAUSMAN
ANDREW REACH
PJ ROGERS

March 10 - May 7, 2016

Presented by
The Artists Archives of the Western Reserve
1834 E 123rd St., Cleveland Ohio 44106

Cover image: Andrew Reach *Diamonds in the Rough* Ultra-chrome Print on Canvas #3/3 54" x 54" 2016

The Artists Archives of the Western Reserve (AAWR) is a unique archival facility and regional museum created to preserve representative bodies of work by Ohio visual artists.

Through ongoing research, exhibition, and educational programs the AAWR actively documents and promotes this cultural heritage for the benefit of the public.

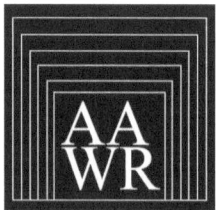

Introduction & Acknowledgments

Reinvention documents the stories of five artists who reinvented themselves and their work in order to overcome limitations forced on them because of traumatic injury, aging or disease. The acceptance, adaptation and growth that each underwent as part of the crisis process resulted in the production of powerful, original bodies of work in divergent directions.

The idea for this show came about through my personal acquaintance with four of the five artists in this exhibition. I have known Ruth Bercaw and Kim Bissett for fifteen years, PJ Rogers for ten years before her death, and Terry Klausman for five years.
I have seen the evolution of all of their work and applauded the outcome. It seemed to me that people could relate to and possibly learn from their individual stories and similar experiences. I am grateful that the AAWR Exhibition Committee approved the idea of this show. While the show was being planned, Board member John Sargent introduced me to the work of Andrew Reach, and in my mind his work perfectly rounds out this exhibition.

In some ways this was not an easy show to curate or install. The artists were chosen for the overall idea of the show rather than obvious shared visual sensibilities. Each of these artists is a perfectionist within their chosen process, but each artist's individual style is very different from the others. The work chosen for this exhibition was also limited by the size of the gallery space. This made it impossible in most cases to really show what each artist had done before the crisis occurred that forced them to change. This is particularly true of the work of Kim Bissett (sculptor) and Andrew Reach (architect). In the case of PJ Rogers and Terry Klausman, who are both extremely prolific, each produced several bodies of work to get from there to here. In this exhibition I can only offer you one piece from each of these separate periods of production, but you should know that each of those works represents many more made at the same time. In Ruth Bercaw's case almost all of her three dimensional, geometric works have been sold to private or corporate collectors, and are unavailable. We were very lucky that Chinese Checkers as well as Gate were still free for exhibition.

I would very much like to thank everyone involved in this undertaking; the artists, the AAWR Board of Directors, The AAWR Exhibition Committee, and our Gallery Coordinator and Archives Assistant Christine Ries. My special thanks to John Sargent for his invaluable help in arranging and installing our AAWR exhibitions. I would also like to thank The Harris Stanton Gallery and The Bonfoey Gallery for lending works on consignment for this exhibition.

My hope as you view this work and read the artists stories in this catalog, is that you will be inspired in your own life. The resiliency of the creative mind to overcome obstacles is something we all can learn from and hope to emulate. It is one of the cornerstones of human evolution and a major reason why the making of art should be encouraged in our culture.

Mindy Tousley
AAWR Executive Director

KIM BISSETT

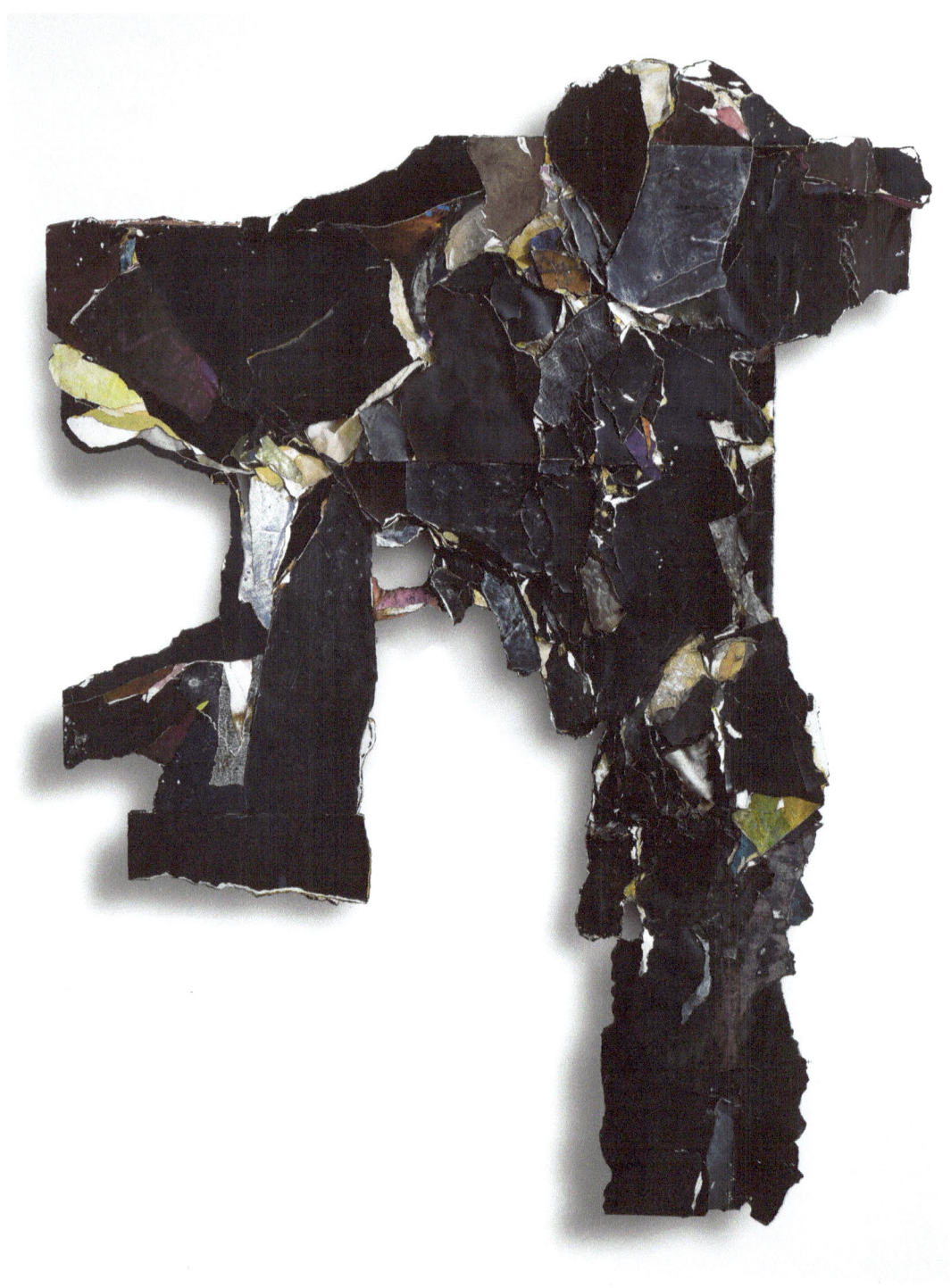

Corpus   mixed media paper relief   90" x 72"

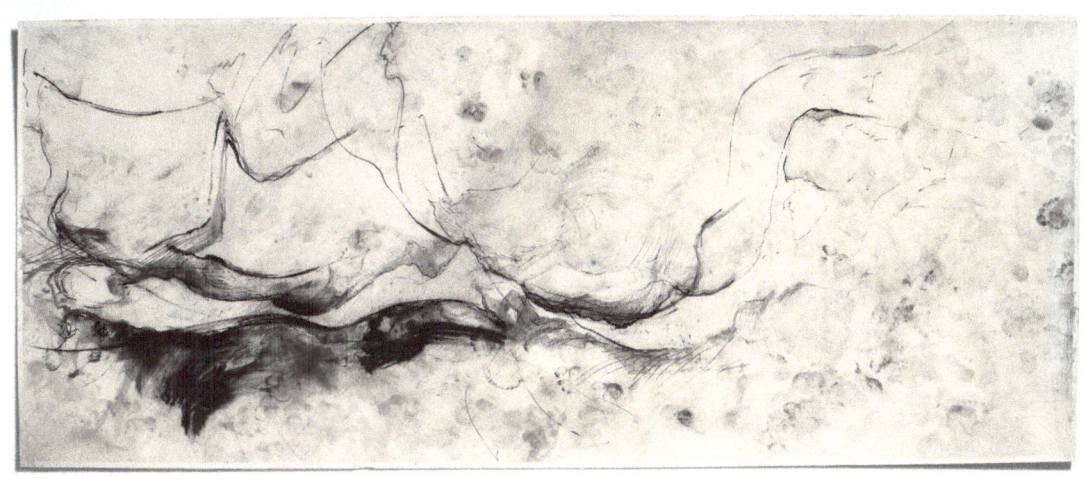

Spring Day 2007 Charcoal & mixed media drawingon paper

In 2005 a profound change occurred in my work when I stopped making sculpture and began making drawings. Nerve damage had made it impossible for me to continue my work in bronze and cast stone. As an artist I was determined to continue to work and communicate. The transition from 3 - D to 2- D space meant learning a new language. I learned how to compress space, set perimeters understand figure/ground relationships, manipulate illusory space, and communicate weight and gravity. My drawings are constructed in a way that relates to my earlier work in sculpture. I layer, laminate, sand, tear, cut, reconfigure, and assemble the paper. The paper allows me immediacy, however that eluded me in sculpture.

Kim Bissett

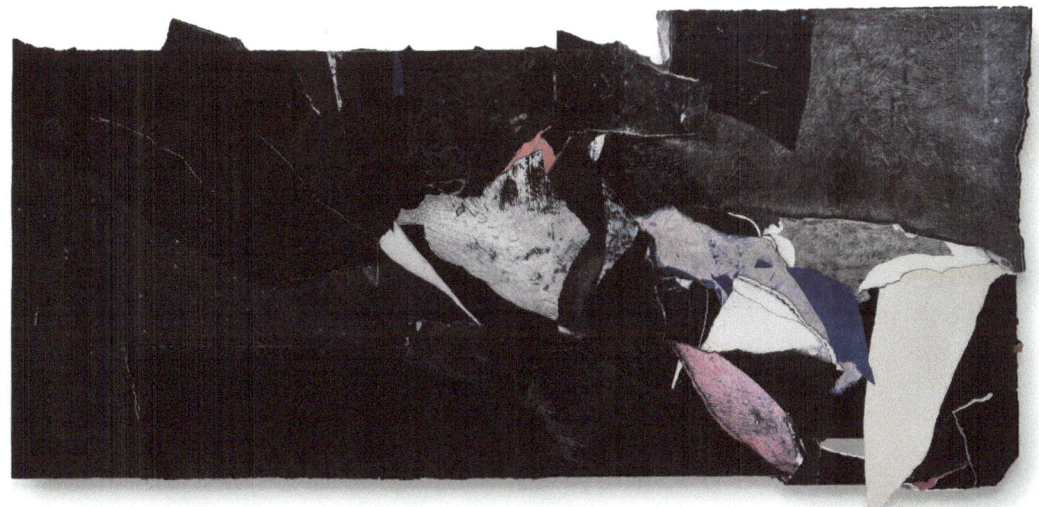

Amistad   mixed media paper relief   38" x 80"

RUTH BERCAW

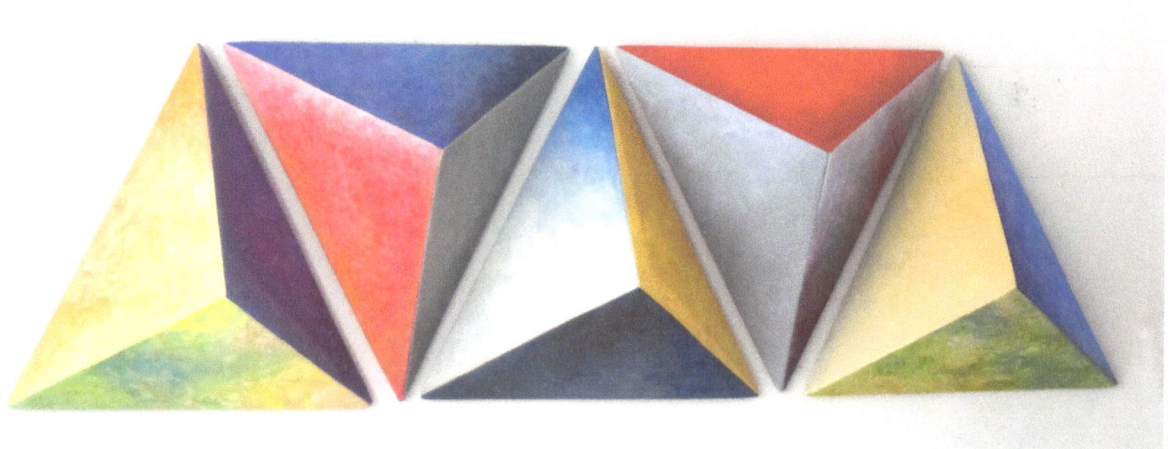

Chinese Checkers oil on constructed canvases   21" x 84.5" x 8.5"

The year was 2005, when I realized that use of the three - dimensional forms which were undeniably popular and distinctively mine would have to be abandoned. Even the smallest of forms was immensely difficult to construct, and building so many of them began to cause pain and swelling in my knuckles and hands. This grew noticeably worse with each new batch. My artistic future did not appear to be entirely impossible, but my spirit was heavy with doubts about my ability to move forward into two dimensions. Such a change would mean leaving behind hard won concepts and a wealth of ideas conceived and developed out of something no longer viable.

Interestingly, adjacent facets of the small forms, themselves mostly color filled and energetic, suggested a way forward. So, really, it was color, lively color, which provided a way out of my perceived dead end and onto a path of invention and optimism. In 2006 my very first works produced on paper were complete surprises to me; they had not lost purpose, but rather were immediately accepted into the exhibition world. Since then, I have worked my way through several series of multimedia paintings, many of them on canvas as well as paper. I have been able to transfer formerly held concepts of evolving life into new phases of artistic expression.

Two recent series of paintings continue my exploration of relationships. One series, rich in abstract imagery, is inspired by observations in a single isolated area of untrammeled woods and covertly alludes to small communities of interests in a never ending, worldwide challenge to evolve and survive. The other series, strongly centered in metaphors involving strata, suggests reflection on past civilizations and entire Eco-systems buried by cycles of catastrophe. Yet, out of it all a selection of things survive and move on. Selected shapes and insistent color represent markers of life.

In the end, for me it seems that enforced change has proven to be a catalyst of new thinking and imagery, a springboard into the future which has included significant art. It has been an outcome to celebrate.

Ruth B.Bercaw

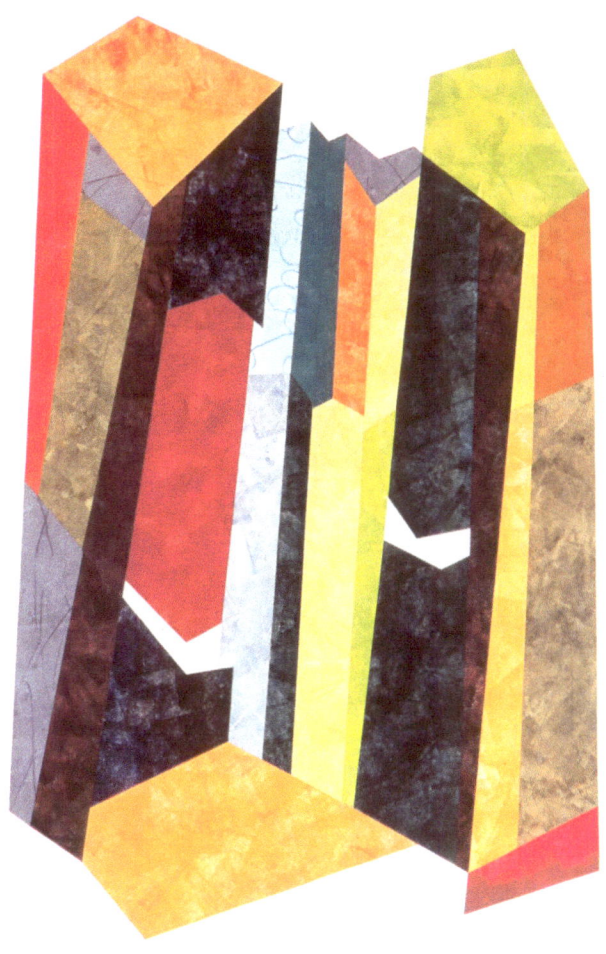

Gate   mixed media on paper   55" x 42.5"

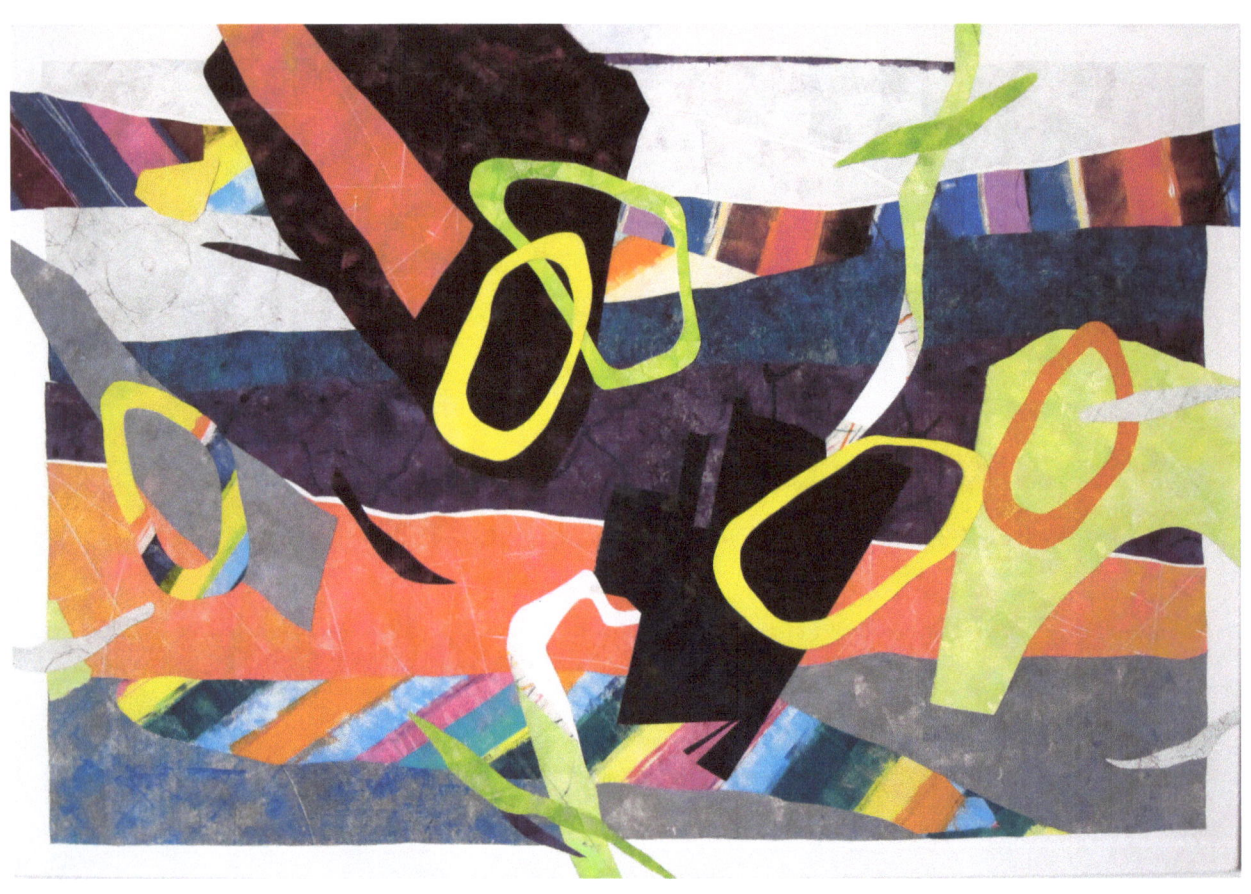

Sounding   mixed media on canvas   40" x 60"

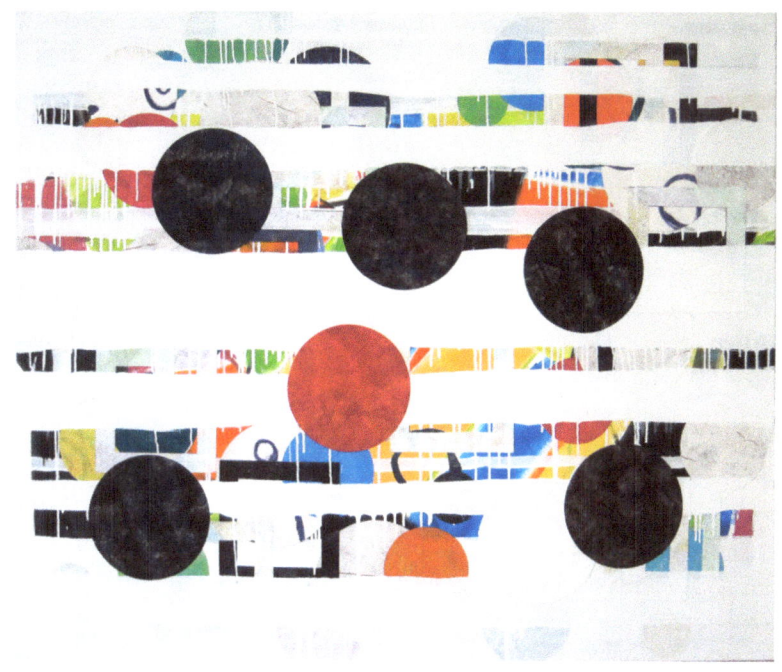

Transported Garden (Tigris)   mixed media on canvas   50" x 58"   2015

Transported Garden (Euphrates)   mixed media on canvas   50" x 58"   2015

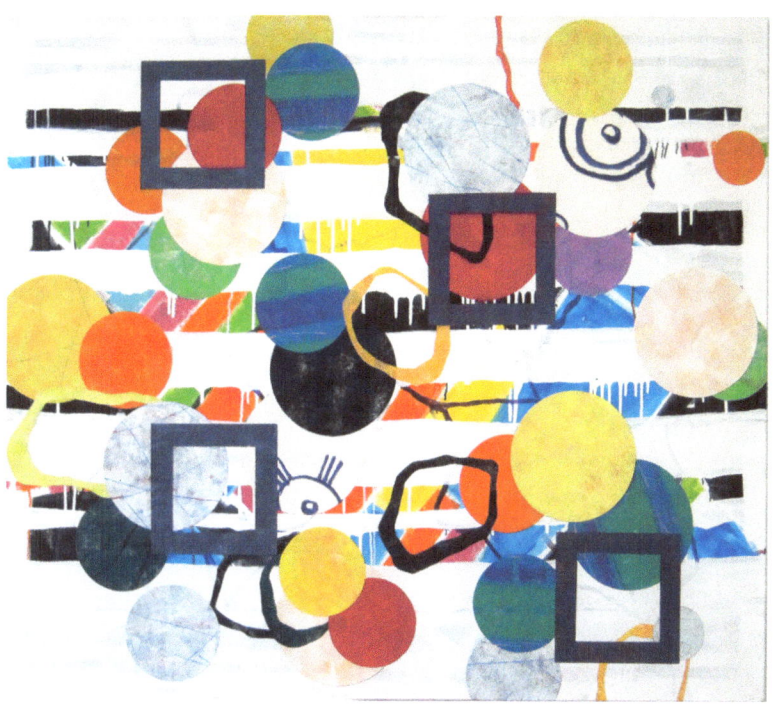

TERRY KLAUSMAN

A welder by trade for the last 20 years, in 2010 I returned to my first love and decided to try my hand at being a professional artist. I am largely self taught but was an award winning artist back in high school. So I began by making fabricated and welded steel sculptures after work. I also began drawing again. I have always loved the feeling of a pencil in my fingers and I began experimenting with Prisma-color pencils. My drawings were unique because I eschewed the common techniques of shading, blending and burnishing in favor of hard edged abstraction. I had become quite prolific and people were beginning to take favorable notice of both the sculpture and the drawings.

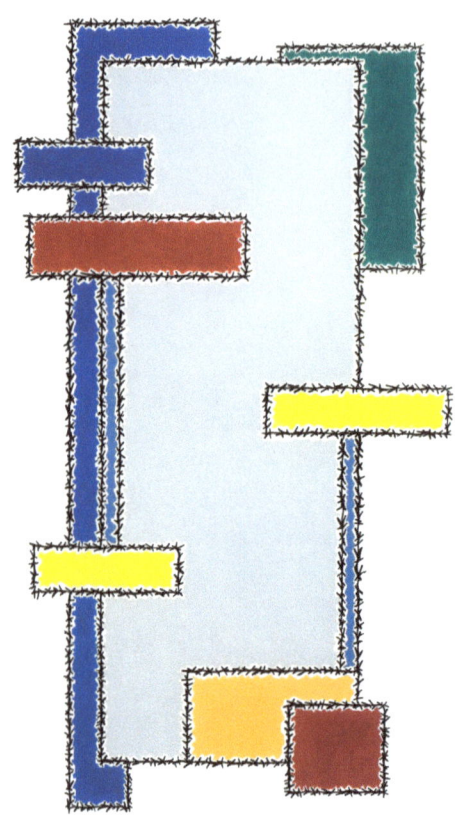

Homage to Mondrian left handed drawing
Prismacolor pencil on paper
23" x 15" 2011

On July 25, 2011 I went to my job as usual and proceeded to work at building a very large steel frame using a crane and lifting clamp to lift into place very large steel plates. While lifting the last piece of steel into place the clamp failed and the steel plate fell on my right hand, my drawing hand. The injury was very severe and after multiple surgeries I was without the use of my right hand for five and one half months. After a short period of feeling sorry for myself I became determined to draw left handed. It would have been impossible to match the precision of my right handed drawing style and so in acknowledgment I created a jagged line to serve as an outline around the solidly colored shapes. There were seven pieces in this series punctuated by my left handed signature at the bottom left of each piece. (Without any forethought, I discovered my signature is virtually identical using either hand). It was while drawing these pieces that I was inspired to make the jagged line the complete subject matter of the next series of drawings.

After regaining use of my right hand, I applied what I had learned from using the left hand and began the exploration of my line. The first drawings were pattern fields typified by symmetrical, non repetitive rows of line in monochrome or polychrome. People began to refer to these as my "barbed wire" or "stitch" drawings. I was satisfied that the line by itself was working well but felt that it needed to be doing something more than just existing in symmetrical rows.

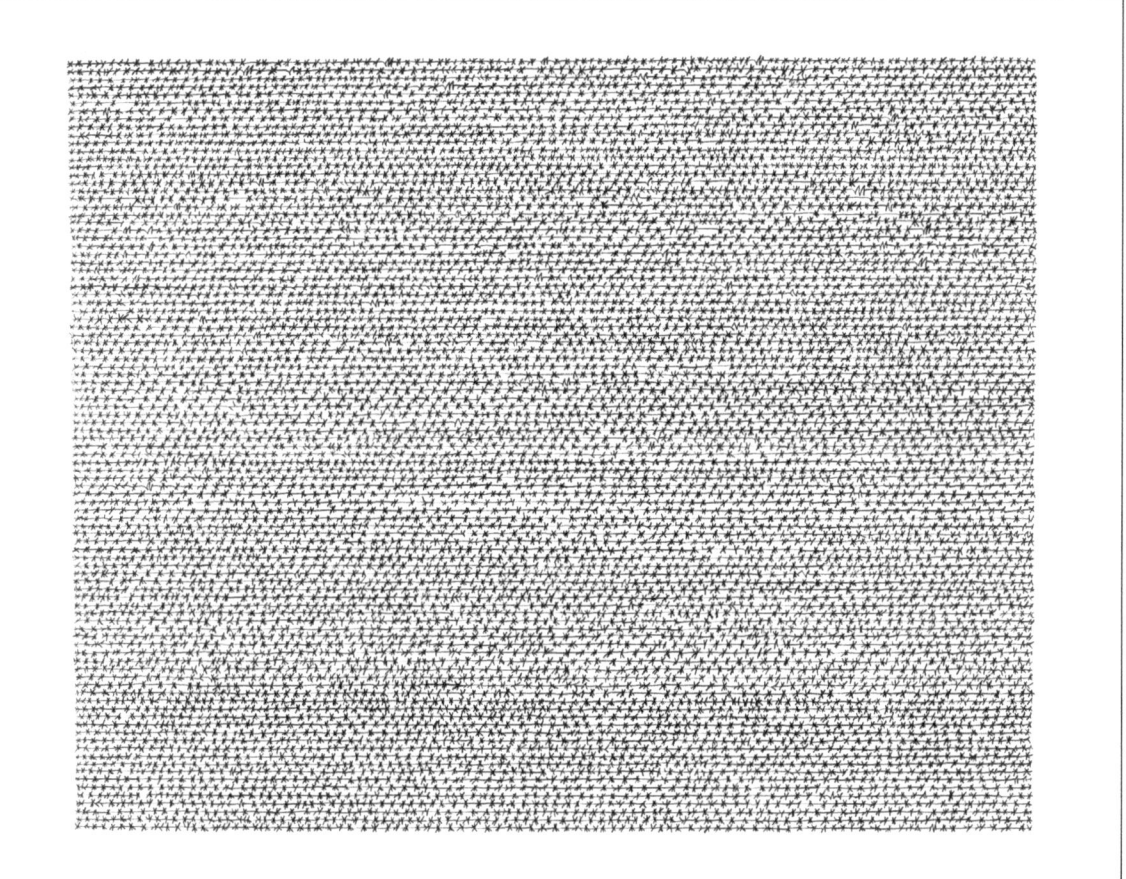

Zen   Prismacolor pencil on paper   32" x 40"   2012

The next series would have the line being pulled apart, ripped, restrained, and tied up. Geometric shapes made their way into the compositions. My work had developed movement and kinetic energy. Although I was very pleased that people had identified my work by a name, "barbed wire", I wanted to make the line softer and more flowing. I was compelled to belie the sharpness of the line and its origins and make work that moved organically like fabric might. Straight lines were replaced with curvilinear, plant - like lines. The work had evolved into something that was the polar opposite of its beginnings.

I now look back on July 25, 2011 as the single most important event in my career as an artist to date. Losing the use of my right hand opened the door to discovery. It forced me to analyze my situation and adapt accordingly using what I was left to work with: my imagination, my talent, and my left hand.

Terry Klausman

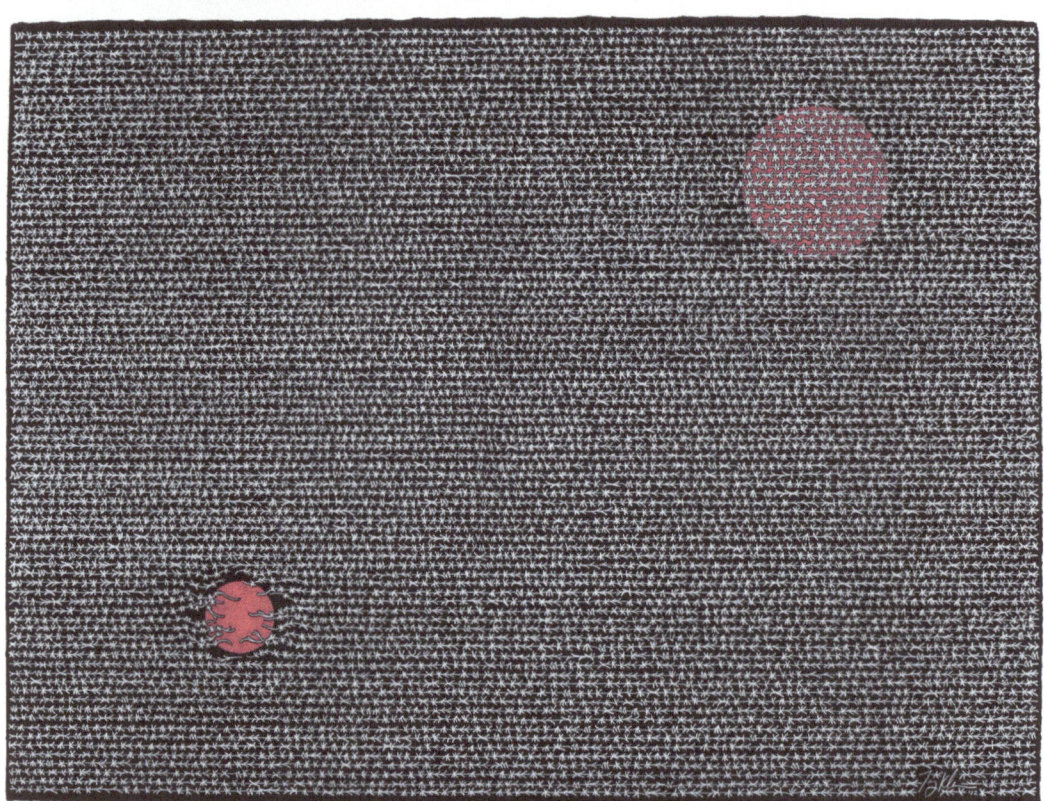

Refection Reversed prisma color pencil on paper   22" x 30"   2012

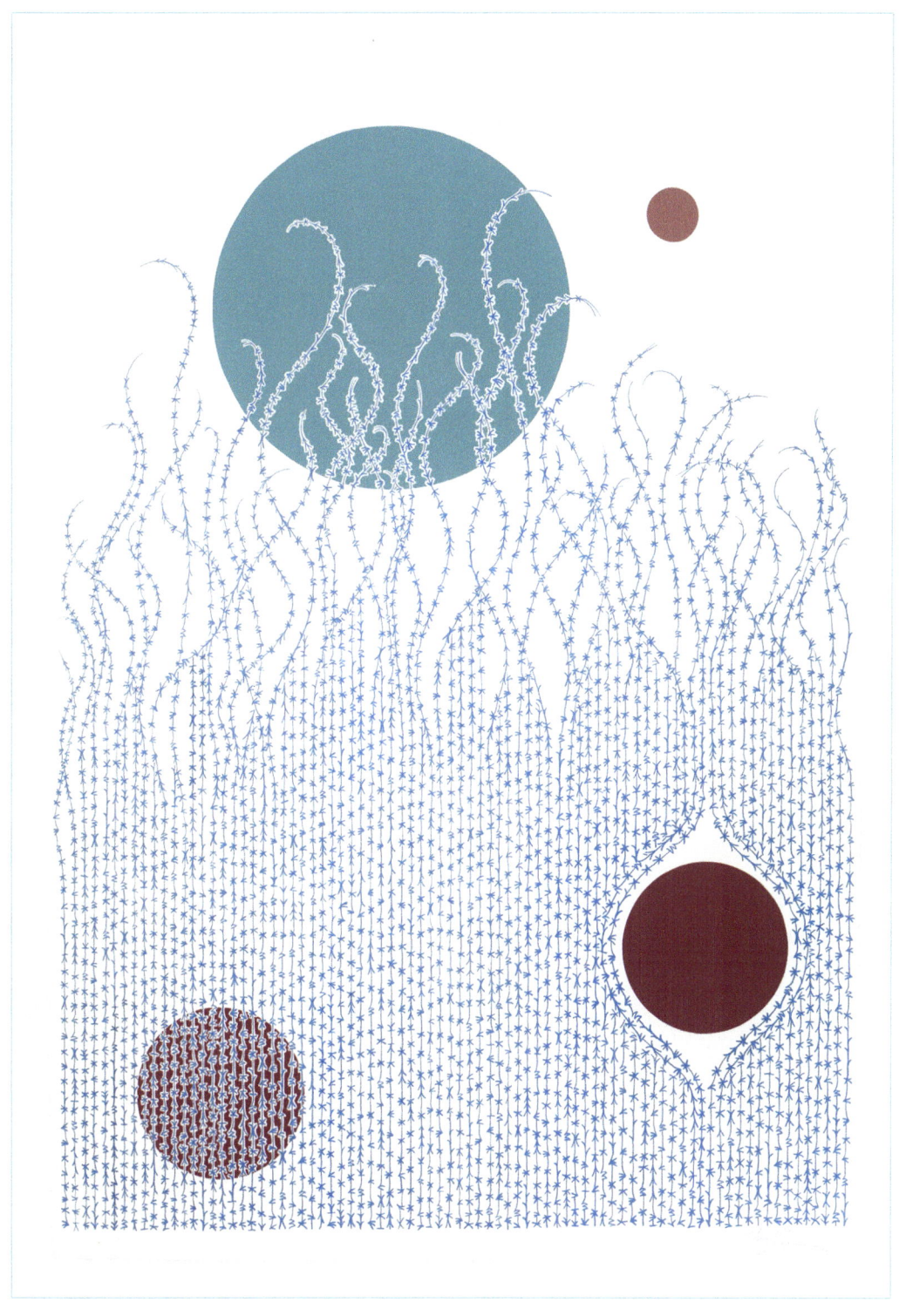

Exposed   Prismacolor pencil on paper   30" x 22"   2013   collection of the Cleveland Clinic

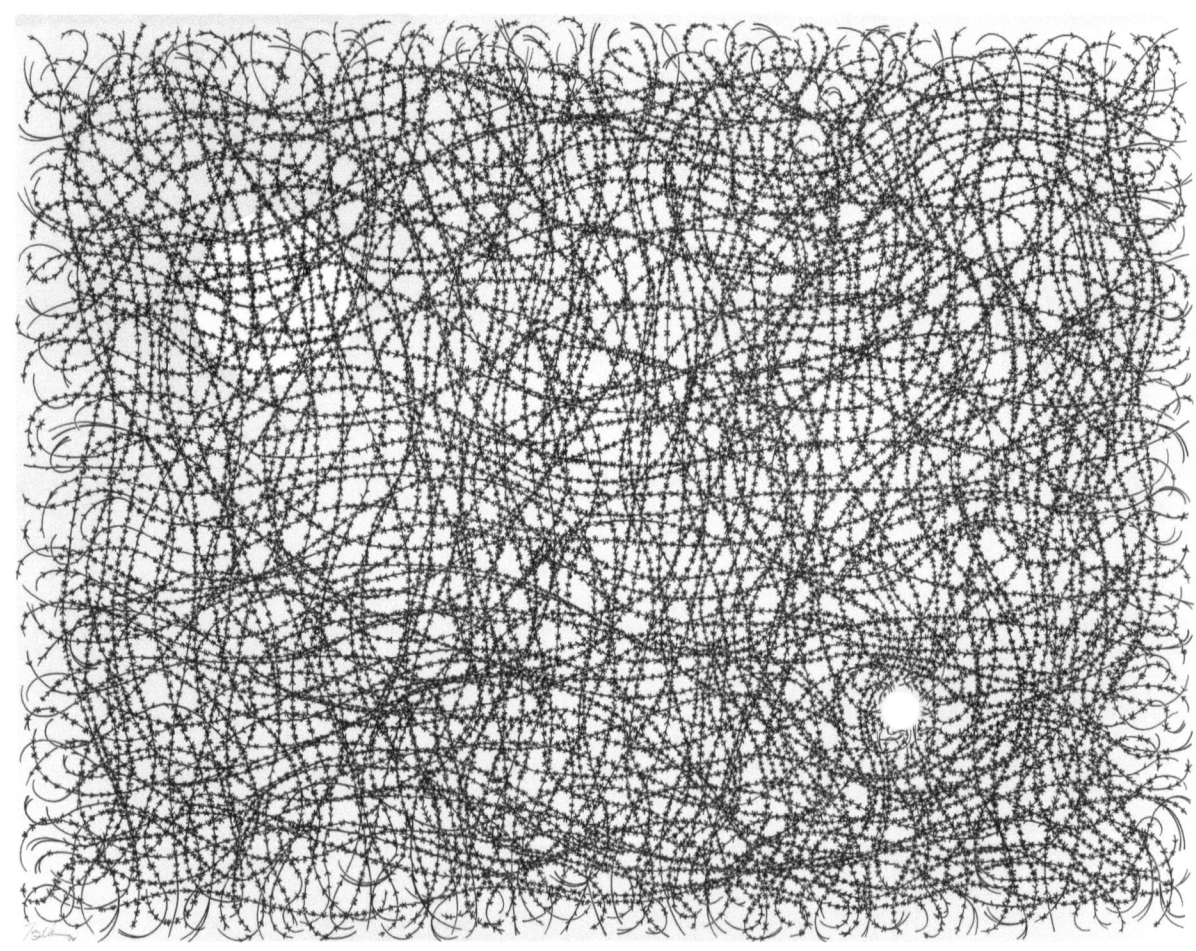

Moonrise Beyond the Thicket   prisma color pencil on paper   22" x 30"   2014

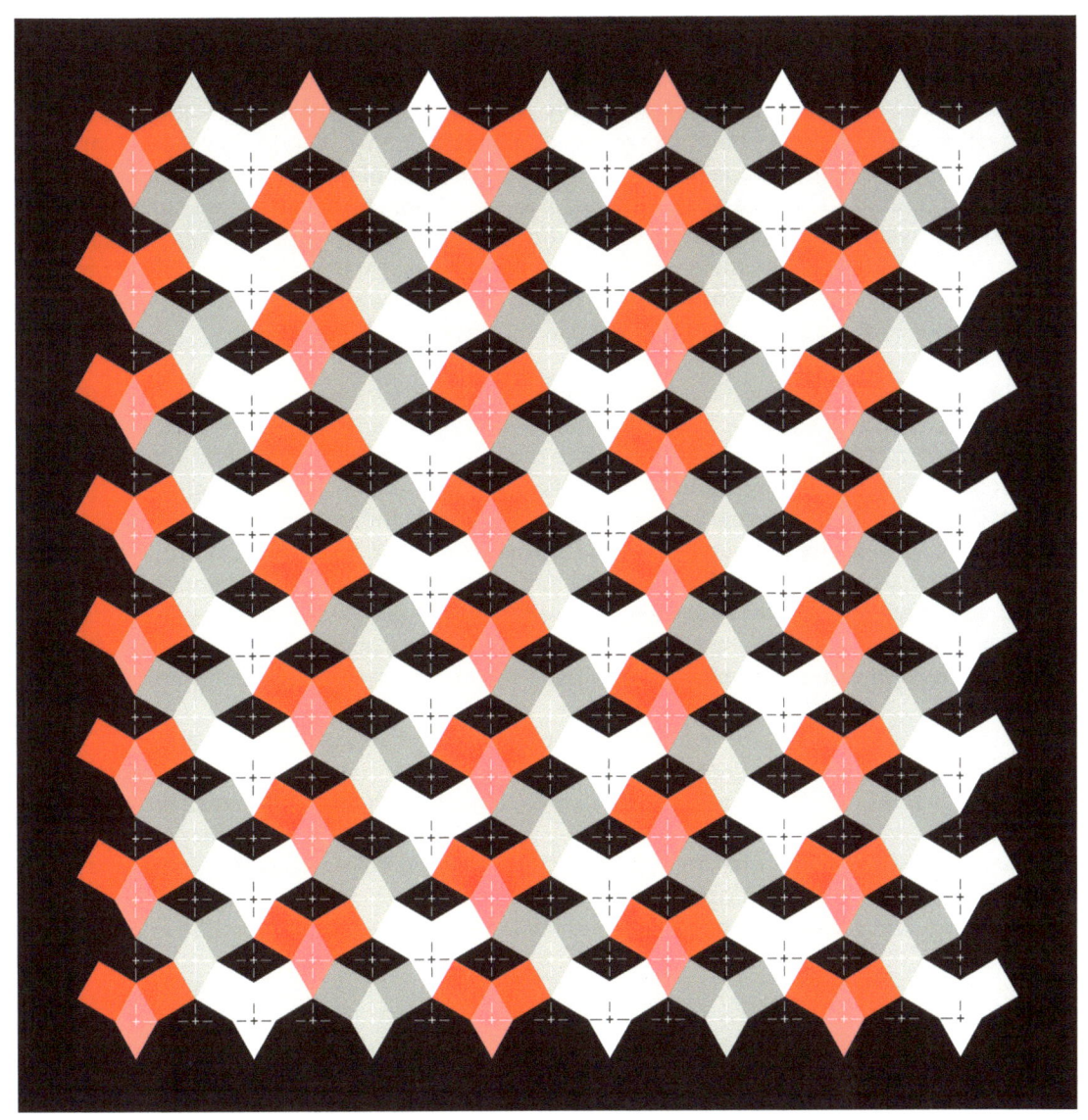

Diamonds in the Rough   Epson Ultrachrome print on canvas 54" x 54"   2016

My generation, the baby boomers, bridged the span between the old analog world and the digital world that would supplant it and this would be an important part of my creative development. As a child I was exposed to architecture when I discovered the blue prints of our house that were buried behind a rack of clothes in my parent's closet. These drawings fascinated me. I was also lucky to have been exposed to modern art as well, through the lithographs of modern artists that hung in our home, and visits to my mother's cousin, who was an art dealer. These experiences started me on a lifelong love of art. She would take me in front of a piece of artwork in her collection and teach me how to see in a way I hadn't before. Fast forward to college where I decided that I would study architecture and my early exposure to modern art would serve me well in learning to design. At that time (1980) architects learned to draft by hand with conventional drafting tools (parallel ruling bar, triangles, protractor, mechanical pencils, rapidograph pens). This was also the time of the birth of CADD (Computer Assisted Design and Drafting). I had the opportunity to be an early adopter of computers in architecture at its earliest stage with a CADD program on a main frame at Pratt's computer lab. Digital technology would progress at a rapid pace with the dawn of the age of the Personal Computer. But as technology progressed, a spine disease also progressed during my 20 years as an architect, leaving me disabled and unable to continue the rigors of practicing architecture.

After a second surgery and severed from my profession, pain took control of me both physically and emotionally and I slipped into a deep depression. Then, at the urging of my life partner Bruce Baumwoll, I began to learn Photoshop. I started to use it to make greeting cards, employing images from Bruce's collection of vintage ephemera. Photoshop was quite different than the CADD software I used in architecture, being a raster program instead of a vector program and required me to adjust to a new way of drawing. The creation of these cards was a transition to what would become making original digital art from scratch. Magically a rich vocabulary of artistic expression began to spring forth. Bruce, seeing something special happening, purchased a large format Epson fine art printer for me. Bruce had an ulterior motive. He helped me print my work and hung them up all around the house to inspire me further and give me hope of a new path for me going forward in my life.

I have come to embrace digital technology to create large format works that would be too physically demanding for me to paint. With Epson Large format fine art printers, I produce my works in editions of three. An outgrowth from my architecture, through geometric abstraction, I'm interested in bridging the realm of the artist and technician and merging these together to create an aesthetic that speaks to modernity in the digital age. Using color and geometric fragments akin to bits, I recombine them, in a visual dance of color, composition and optic play to imbue in them a kinetic sense of movement; a stand in for my inability to move freely through the world without pain.

As I contemplate what it means to be human in today's technological world, I embrace technology to help me express myself and have a voice. For me, digitally created art must be rendered as a physical print to make it a tangible instead of a virtual object, thus bringing the digital back to the analog in the age old custom of hanging a picture on the wall to be viewed and appreciated as an object of beauty, something that a computer screen cannot match.

Andrew Reach

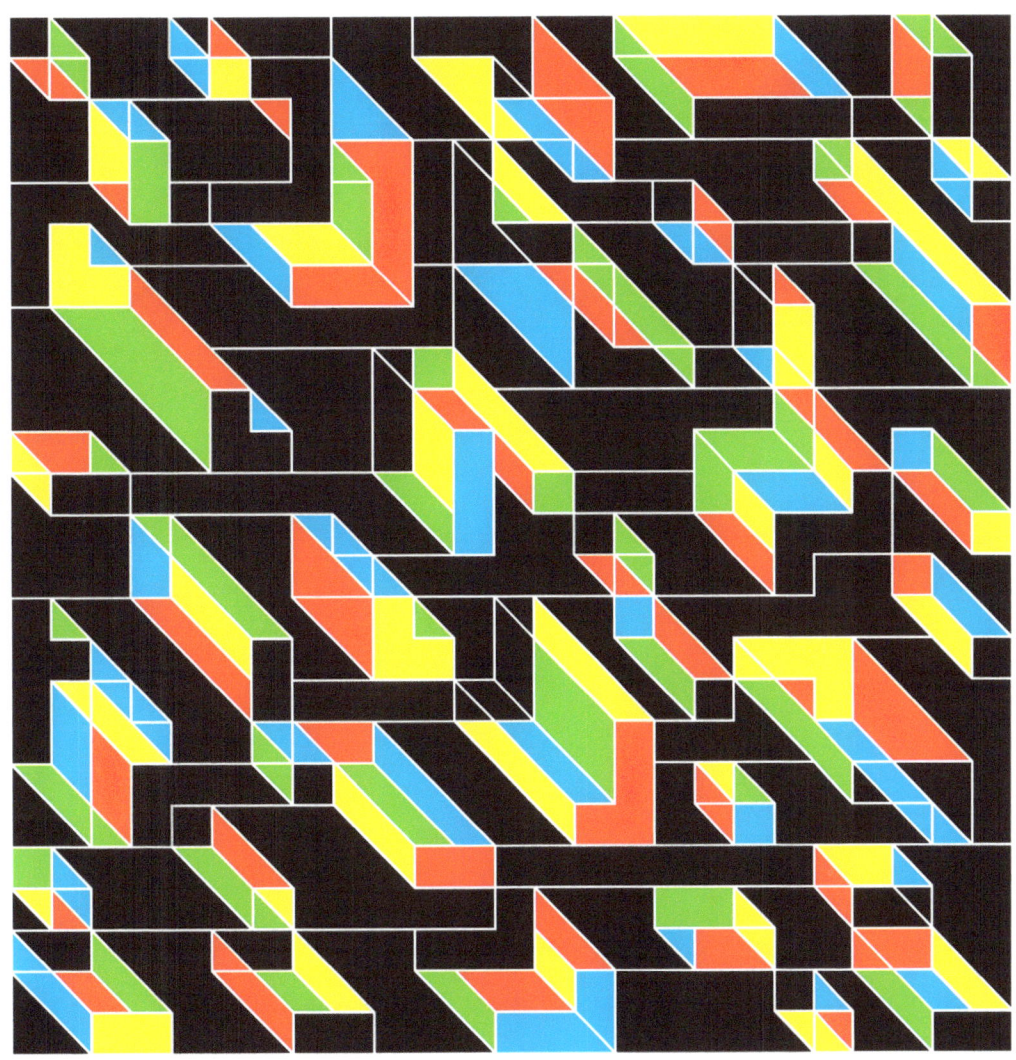

Solid Ambiguities Epson Ultrachrome print on canvas   50" x 50" 2016

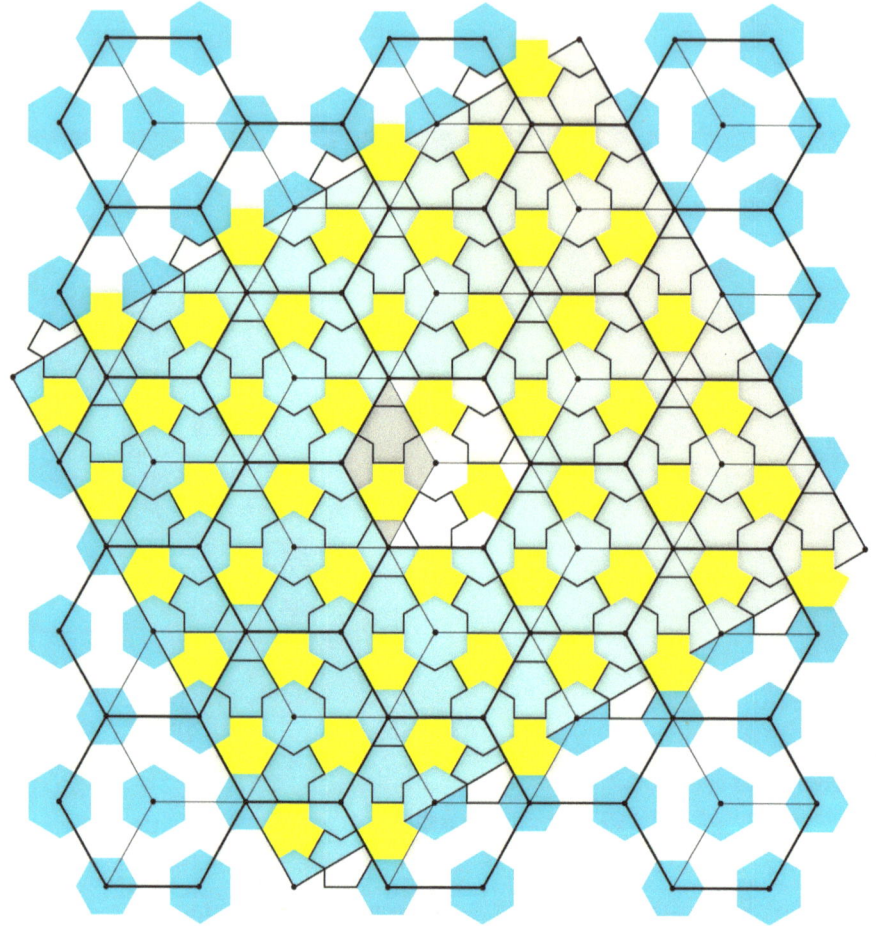

Construct O45.15   Epson Ultrachrome print on cotton rag paper #2/3   46.75" x 44"

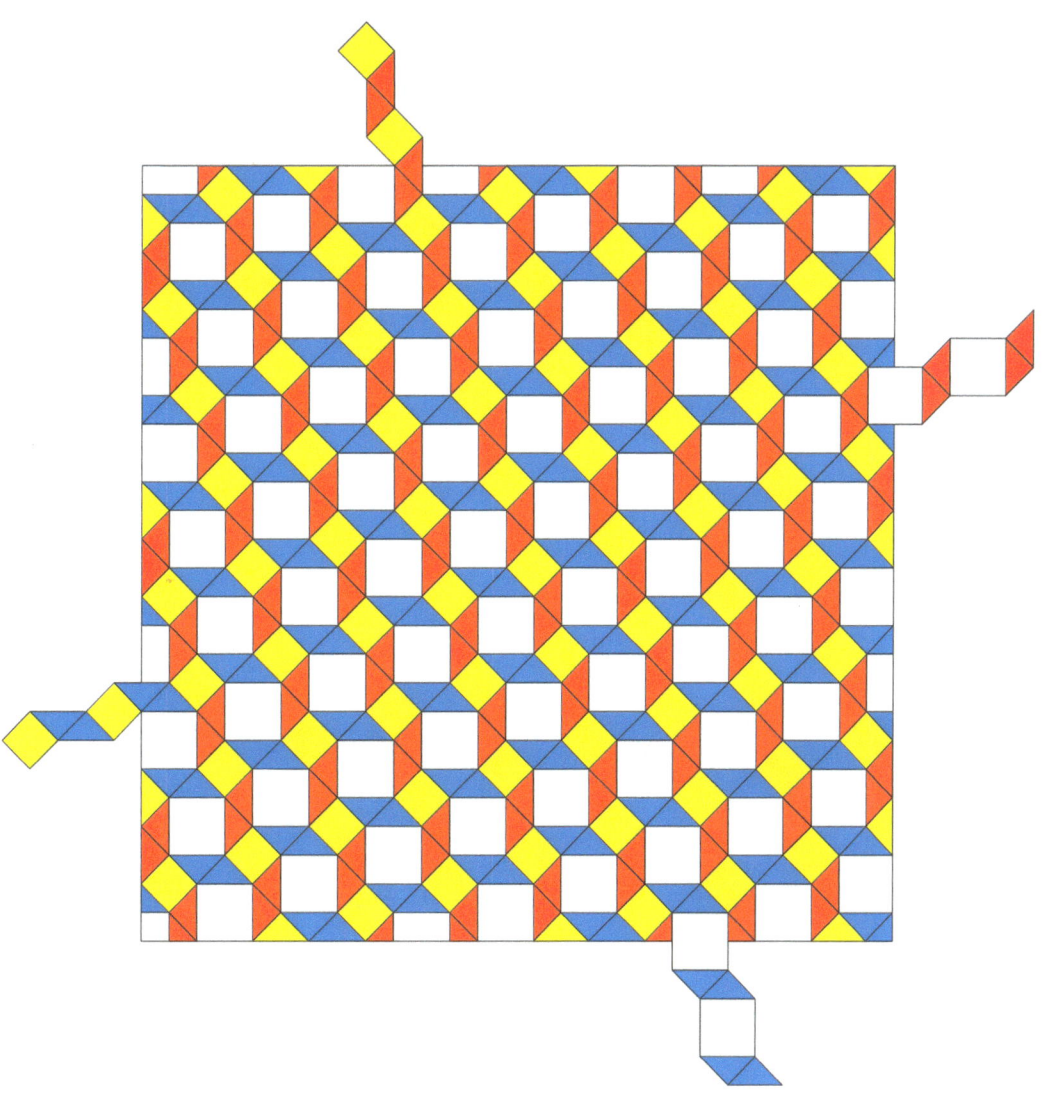

Four   Epson Ultrachrome   print on cotton rag paper #2/3   44" x 44"   2016

PJ ROGERS (1925 - 2014)

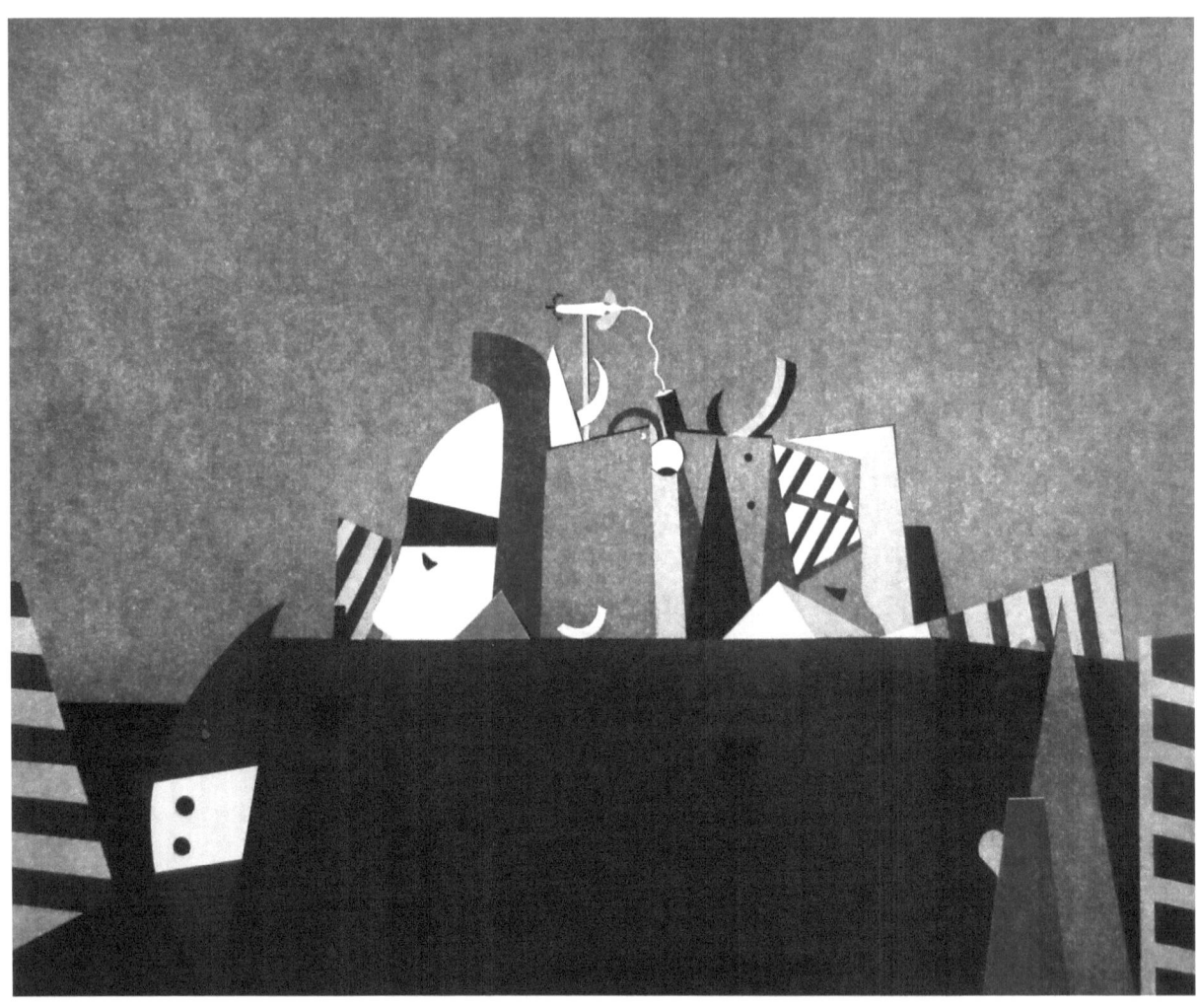

Lure II   aquatint with collage on paper   22" x 30" #2/20 circa 1980's

Before PJ Rogers became known as a printmaker, she was a successful sculptor and painter receiving several commissions for portraits of notable Akron leaders. Gradually she became interested in printmaking and explored making woodcuts. In the early 1970's she attended a show of aquatints and became so fascinated by the medium that she began to teach herself the process.

She developed an amazing feel for the medium as well as impressive technical skills. Of this work PJ writes, "...I seek the Life that is beneath but parallel to the superficial. I am interested in transparency, meaning the stripping away of the superficial to understand the core – the gradual breakdown of forms and feelings – to understand – absorbed into blackness (the mass of all particles) and reflected back as the cycle begins anew. Aquatint is the appropriate medium with which to express this, as it is a transparent medium of greatest contrasts." This body of work represented by the aquatints from the 1980's, has been highly acclaimed nationally and universally accepted for its excellence.

In 1988, the year her husband died, Rogers realized that she had become severely allergic to the inks and solvents used in the aquatints. She could no longer practice the craft of traditional printmaking and so she had to reinvent herself as an artist. After acquiring a second hand Polaroid camera at a flea market she began photographing and manipulating images (by drawing on the film as it develops), and printing them as electrostatic collages. The body of work produced during the period from 1988 to the late1990's transitions into the work that Rogers would produce until her death in 2014.

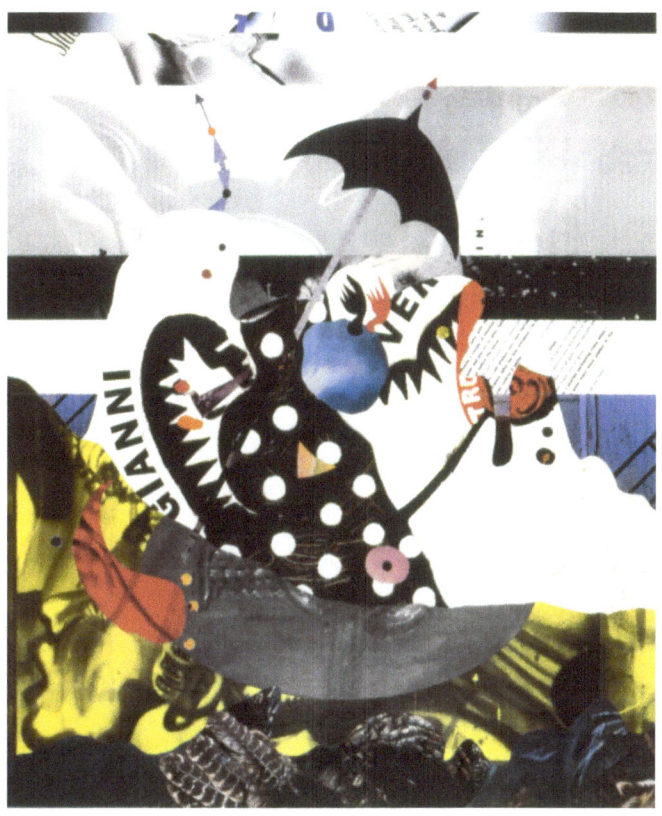

I Clasp My Umbrella Firmly   electrostatic print, collage on paper #1/3   30" x 22"

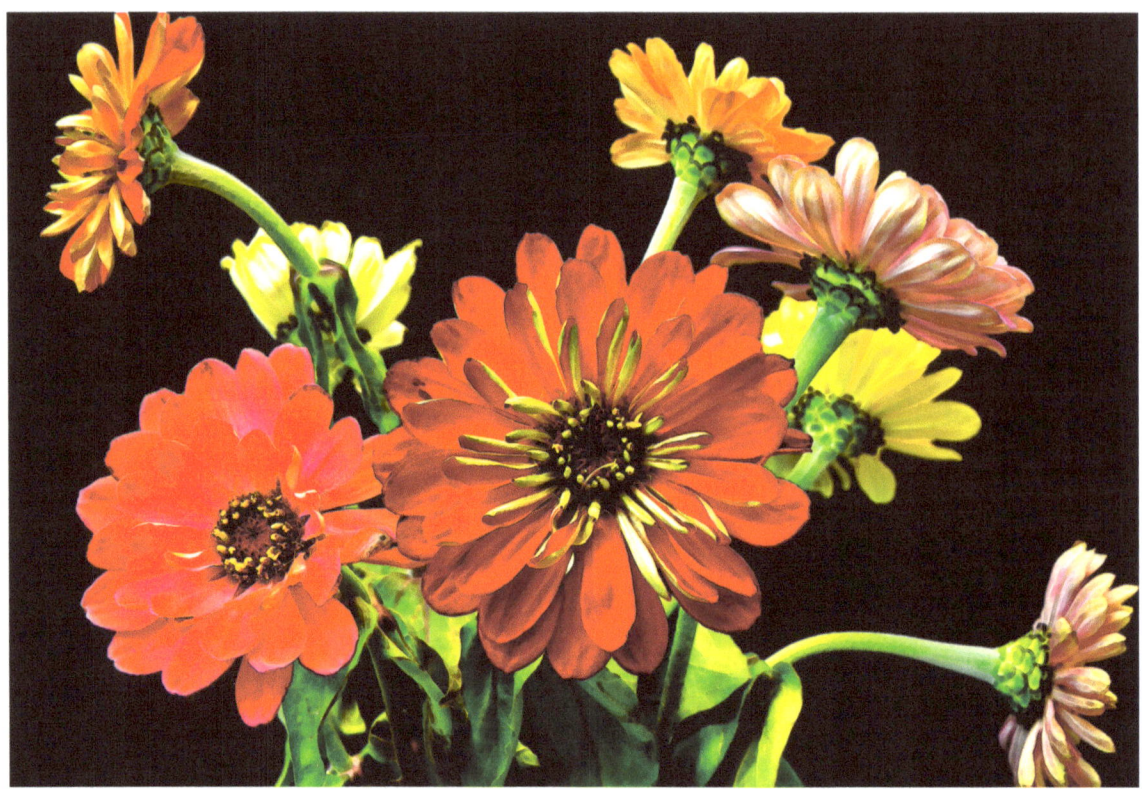

Zinnias I archival inkjet mono print on paper   20" x 16"   circa 2011

As personal computers became more available and affordable for individuals to use, Rogers began seriously considering this as a tool for making art. By 2001 she had bought her first computer and began playing with digital photographs of flowers and other forms from nature and manipulating them using the software that came with her mac. The dense black behind the simple botanicals was never part of the original photograph but was achieved solely on the computer and served as a stand in for the blacks of her aquatints. By 2004 she had mastered Photoshop and was extensively reworking images by manipulating, color shifting, outlining, clipping and using various filters as well as multiple layers to create digital prints. She considered the computer a tool just as a paint brush would be and often referred to her digital images as being "painted with a computer".

The underlying ideas beneath the surface qualities of her digital work involve the concept of time and how we as humans experience time as a montage of transitory stimuli layered together continuously. She writes, "I wish to express change and movement and the idea that time is made up of the overlapping of many small moments". These ideas are consistent ties that bind together all of her work from the past 40 plus years. Throughout her life PJ pushed the boundaries of the medium that she chose to work in at any given time. Remarkably, she mastered the extremely difficult technical artistic skills of traditional printmaking and then of modern computer technology on her own. Beyond the technical mastery she displays in her finished work is the consistent way she used those skills to express her ideas about art and life.

Mindy Tousley

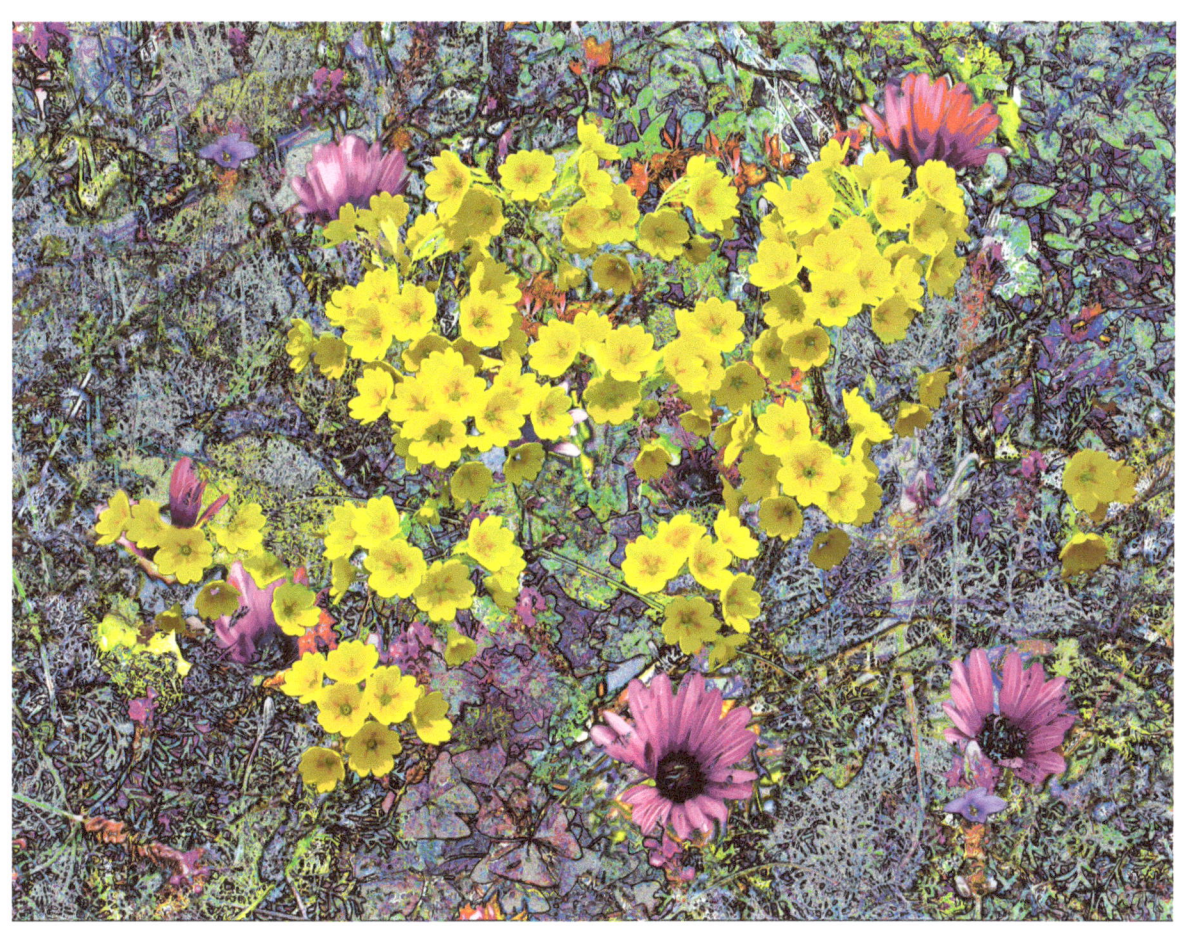

Layers of Time in the Garden 4   archival inkjet pigment print on paper   36" x 45"   #2/10 circa 2012

www.ingramcontent.com/pod-product-compliance
Lightning Source LLC
Chambersburg PA
CBHW050912180526
45159CB00007B/2886